Abo[ut] Skill Builders Division

by Jessica Breur

Welcome to RBP Books' Skill Builders series. Like our Summer Bridge Activities collection, the Skill Builders series is designed to make learning both fun and rewarding.

Skill Builders Division provides students with focused practice to help them reinforce and develop division skills. Each Skill Builders volume is grade-level appropriate, with clear examples and instructions to guide the lessons. Skill Builders Division combines a number of approaches and activities to help introduce students to basic division facts from 1 to 12, dividing with and without remainders, beginning long division, and use of division in life skills.

A critical thinking section includes exercises to help develop higher order thinking skills.

Learning is more effective when approached with an element of fun and enthusiasm—just as most children approach life. That's why the Skill Builders combine entertaining and academically sound exercises with eye-catching graphics and fun themes—to make reviewing basic skills fun and effective, for both you and your budding scholars.

www.summerbridgeactivities.com

Table of Contents

Introduction

Division problems can be written three different ways.

A. The most common way is $3\overline{)15}$

You write the answer above the large number: $\begin{array}{r} 5 \\ 3\overline{)15} \end{array}$

Examples:

$\begin{array}{r} 5 \\ 6\overline{)30} \end{array}$ $\begin{array}{r} 6 \\ 4\overline{)24} \end{array}$ $\begin{array}{r} 6 \\ 8\overline{)48} \end{array}$ $\begin{array}{r} 5 \\ 5\overline{)25} \end{array}$

B. Another common way is horizontally: $15 \div 3$

The answer is written at the end: $15 \div 3 = 5$

Examples:

$18 \div 3 = 6$ $28 \div 7 = 4$ $66 \div 6 = 11$

C. The third way to write a division problem looks like a fraction. It can also be called an **improper fraction** because the largest number is on top. The top number is called the **numerator** in a fraction. It is called a **dividend** in division.

$\frac{15}{3}$ The answer is put on the right: $\frac{15}{3} = 5$

Examples:

$\frac{24}{4} = 6$ $\frac{28}{7} = 4$ $\frac{48}{8} = 6$

Throughout this workbook you may see problems written these three different ways.

Introduction

Division is breaking a big number into a smaller number. Each number in a division problem has a special name.

A. The number you divide into parts is the **dividend**. (This is the biggest number.)

$6\overline{)24}$ = 4 ← **Dividend**

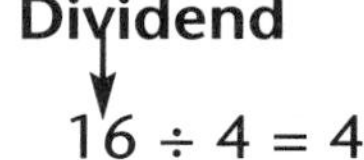

$\frac{18}{3} = 6$ ← **Dividend**

B. The number you divide by is the **divisor**.

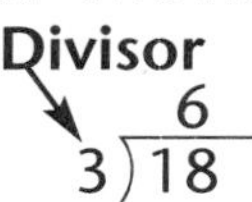

$3\overline{)18}$ = 6 (**Divisor** → 3)

$27 \div 9 = 3$ (**Divisor** → 9)

$\frac{12}{4} = 3$ (**Divisor** → 4)

C. The answer is also called a **quotient**.

$3\overline{)9}$ = 3 ← **Quotient**

$20 \div 5 = 4$ (**Quotient** → 4)

$\frac{21}{3} = 7$ ← **Quotient**

The following problems are solved for you. Practice labeling the **quotient**, **divisor**, and **dividend** in these division problems.

1. 10 ÷ 2 = **5**
5 is the quotient

2. **18** ÷ 3 = 6
18 is the ____________

3. **16** ÷ 8 = 2
16 is the ____________

4. 30 ÷ **6** = 5
6 is the ____________

5. 27 ÷ 3 = **9**
9 is the ____________

6. **42** ÷ 6 = 7
42 is the ____________

7. 32 ÷ **8** = 4
8 is the ____________

8. 21 ÷ 3 = **7**
7 is the ____________

Introduction

You can use pictures to help you find a **quotient** to a division problem.

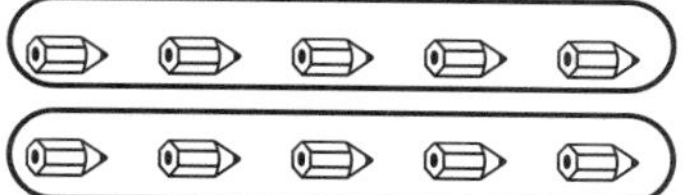

1 group

2 groups

$10 \div 2 = 5$

Use the **divisor** to divide the pictures into groups. In this case, you need two groups. Then count how many are in each group. That is the **quotient**.

Try some on your own. Draw pictures to help you.

1. $18 \div 3 =$ 6

2. $9 \div 1 =$ _____

3. $20 \div 4 =$ _____

4. $12 \div 3 =$ _____

5. $14 \div 7 =$ _____

6. $6 \div 2 =$ _____

7. $24 \div 6$ _____

8. $15 \div 5 =$ _____

Introduction

Here is another way to use pictures to help you.

10 ÷ 2 = 5  2 in each circle

This time use the **divisor** to divide, or circle, each picture into groups with the same number as the divisor. For this picture, you will circle groups of 2. Then count your circles. The number of circles is the **quotient**.

Try some on your own using this method.

1. 20 ÷ 5 = 4

2. 18 ÷ 3 = _____

✖ ✖ ✖ ✖ ✖ ✖
✖ ✖ ✖ ✖ ✖ ✖
✖ ✖ ✖ ✖ ✖ ✖

3. 4 ÷ 4 = _____

✏ ✏ ✏ ✏

4. 21 ÷ 7 = _____

☆ ☆ ☆ ☆ ☆ ☆ ☆
☆ ☆ ☆ ☆ ☆ ☆ ☆
☆ ☆ ☆ ☆ ☆ ☆ ☆

5. 16 ÷ 8 = _____

6. 15 ÷ 3 = _____

7. 10 ÷ 5 = _____

8. 12 ÷ 4 = _____

Have Some Fun with Number 1

When dividing by 1, the quotient is always the same as the dividend because you are putting the dividend into 1 group.

Find the quotient for each problem. Use pictures if you need to.

1. 2 ÷ 1 = 2

2. 11 ÷ 1 = ______ ☆ ☆ ☆ ☆ ☆ ☆ ☆ ☆ ☆ ☆ ☆

3. 6 ÷ 1 = ______

4. 8 ÷ 1 = ______

5. 5 ÷ 1 = ______

6. 10 ÷ 1 = ______

7. 3 ÷ 1 = ______

8. 7 ÷ 1 = ______

9. 9 ÷ 1 = ______

10. 4 ÷ 1 = ______

11. 12 ÷ 1 = ______

Dividing by 2 Is Easy to Do

When dividing by 2, you are really just dividing a number in half. This is because you are putting the dividend into 2 groups.

Find the quotient for each problem. Use pictures if you need to.

1. 6 pencils ÷ 2 = ___3___

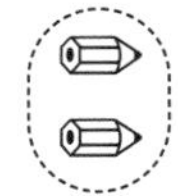 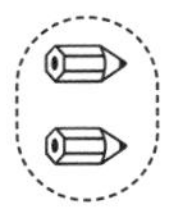 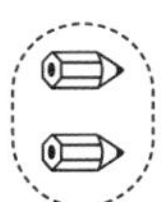

2. 4 flowers ÷ 2 = ______

3. 10 phones ÷ 2 = ______

4. 16 forks ÷ 2 = ______

5. 2 stars ÷ 2 = ______

6. 12 fish ÷ 2 = ______

7. 14 oranges ÷ 2 = ______

8. 8 candies ÷ 2 = ______

9. 18 bowling pins ÷ 2 = ______

10. 20 spiders ÷ 2 = ______

Dividing by 2

Find the quotient. The divisor is 2 in all the problems.

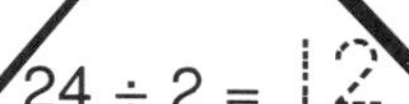

24 ÷ 2 = 12

2 ÷ 2 = ______

8 ÷ 2 = ______

14 ÷ 2 = ______

6 ÷ 2 = ______

18 ÷ 2 = ______

$2\overline{)10}$ = ______

$2\overline{)20}$ = ______

$2\overline{)12}$ = ______

$2\overline{)4}$ = ______

$2\overline{)14}$ = ______

$2\overline{)18}$ = ______

$\frac{2}{2}$ = ______

$\frac{12}{2}$ = ______

$\frac{24}{2}$ = ______

$\frac{6}{2}$ = ______

$\frac{22}{2}$ = ______

Dividing by 3

Put pictures into 3 groups to help find the quotient.

1. 18 ÷ 3 = 6

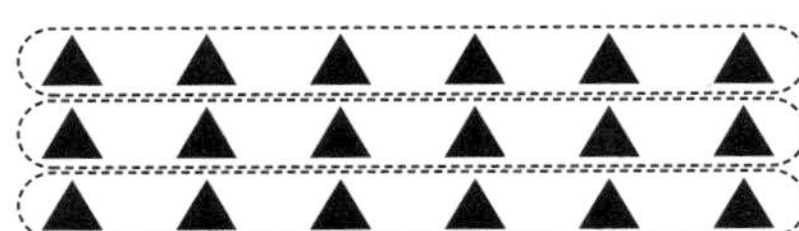

2. 6 ÷ 3 = ______

✤ ✤ ✤ ✤ ✤ ✤

3. 15 ÷ 3 = ______

✚ ✚ ✚ ✚ ✚ ✚ ✚ ✚ ✚
✚ ✚ ✚ ✚ ✚ ✚

4. 9 ÷ 3 = ______

5. 3 ÷ 3 = ______

6. 12 ÷ 3 = ______

7. 30 ÷ 3 = ______

8. 21 ÷ 3 = ______

Dividing by 3

Test your ability to divide by 3 on the three bears.

$3 \div 3 =$ 1

$12 \div 3 =$ ______

$21 \div 3 =$ ______

$15 \div 3 =$ ______

$9 \div 3 =$ ______

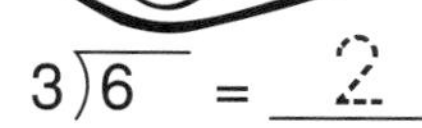

$3\overline{)6} =$ 2

$3\overline{)15} =$ ______

$3\overline{)24} =$ ______

$3\overline{)12} =$ ______

$3\overline{)3} =$ ______

$\frac{9}{3} =$ 3

$\frac{18}{3} =$ ______

$\frac{27}{3} =$ ______

$\frac{6}{3} =$ ______

$\frac{30}{3} =$ ______

Review division facts 1–3

Draw a line from the division problem to the correct picture.

1. 9 ÷ 3 = ______ A. ▲▲▲▲▲ / ▲▲▲▲▲ / ▲▲▲▲▲

2. 12 ÷ 2 = ______ B. ✻ ✻ ✻ ✻ ✻

3. 10 ÷ 2 = ______ C. ▲▲▲ / ▲▲▲ / ▲▲▲

4. 15 ÷ 3 = ______ D. ✻ ✻ ✻ ✻ ✻ / ✻ ✻ ✻ ✻ ✻

5. 5 ÷ 1 = ______ E. ▲▲▲▲▲▲ / ▲▲▲▲▲▲

Now draw your own pictures to show the quotient for the following problems.

6. 12 ÷ 3 = ______

7. 4 ÷ 1 = ______

8. 8 ÷ 2 = ______

9. 18 ÷ 3 = ______

10. 6 ÷ 1 = ______

Word Problems

Find the quotients.

Matt has 24 cookies to share with 3 friends. How many cookies will each friend get?

24 ÷ 3 = 8 cookies

1. Jake has 12 stuffed animals to put onto 2 shelves. He puts the same number of animals on each shelf. How many animals are on each shelf?

2. Matt has 9 baseball cards to give to 3 friends. If he gives the same number to each friend, how many cards will each friend get?

3. Emily has 10 kittens. She has 2 dishes to feed the kittens with. How many kittens will eat at a dish so there is an equal number at each dish?

4. Joy saw 14 rabbits in 2 different cages. If there were the same number in each cage, how many rabbits were in each cage?

Dividing by 4

Use pictures to help you find the basic facts for dividing by 4.

1. $4 \div 4 =$ ______

2. $12 \div 4 =$ ______

3. $24 \div 4 =$ ______

4. $20 \div 4 =$ ______

5. $8 \div 4 =$ ______

6. $32 \div 4 =$ ______

7. $16 \div 4 =$ ______

8. $44 \div 4 =$ ______

9. $28 \div 4 =$ ______

10. $36 \div 4 =$ ______

11. $40 \div 4 =$ ______

12. $48 \div 4 =$ ______

Four Flower Power

Write the quotient for each problem in its flower.

1. $12 \div 4 =$ $36 \div 4 =$ $4 \div 4 =$ $20 \div 4 =$

2. $8 \div 4 =$ $44 \div 4 =$ $28 \div 4 =$ $16 \div 4 =$

3. $24 \div 4 =$ $4 \div 4 =$ $36 \div 4 =$ $32 \div 4 =$

4. $40 \div 4 =$ $48 \div 4 =$ $12 \div 4 =$ $8 \div 4 =$

Dividing by 5

<u>Hint</u>: You can use pictures, or count by 5's until you get to the dividend. The number of times you count by 5 is your quotient.

Example: 30 ÷ 5

Count <u>5</u>, <u>10</u>, <u>15</u>, <u>20</u>, <u>25</u>, <u>30</u>. We counted 6 numbers, so the quotient is 6.

1. 5 ÷ 5 = __1__

2. 30 ÷ 5 = ______

3. 20 ÷ 5 = ______

4. 10 ÷ 5 = ______

5. 35 ÷ 5 = ______

6. 45 ÷ 5 = ______

7. 55 ÷ 5 = ______

8. 60 ÷ 5 = ______

9. 15 ÷ 5 = ______

10. 25 ÷ 5 = ______

5's in the Hive

Find the quotients for 5 in the hive.

1. 20 ÷ 5 = 4

2. 60 ÷ 5 = ______
3. 30 ÷ 5 = ______

4. 20 ÷ 5 = ______
5. 25 ÷ 5 = ______

6. 45 ÷ 5 = ______
7. 35 ÷ 5 = ______

8. 5 ÷ 5 = ______
9. 40 ÷ 5 = ______

10. 10 ÷ 5 = ______
11. 50 ÷ 5 = ______

12. 15 ÷ 5 = ______
13. 55 ÷ 5 = ______

You're doing a honey of a job!

Dividing by 6

Use pictures to help you divide by 6.

1. $6 \div 6 =$ ______

2. $36 \div 6 =$ ______

3. $48 \div 6 =$ ______

4. $18 \div 6 =$ ______

5. $30 \div 6 =$ ______

6. $60 \div 6 =$ ______

7. $66 \div 6 =$ ______

8. $12 \div 6 =$ ______

9. $24 \div 6 =$ ______

10. $54 \div 6 =$ ______

11. $42 \div 6 =$ ______

12. $72 \div 6 =$ ______

Six Really Kicks!

Solve each problem.

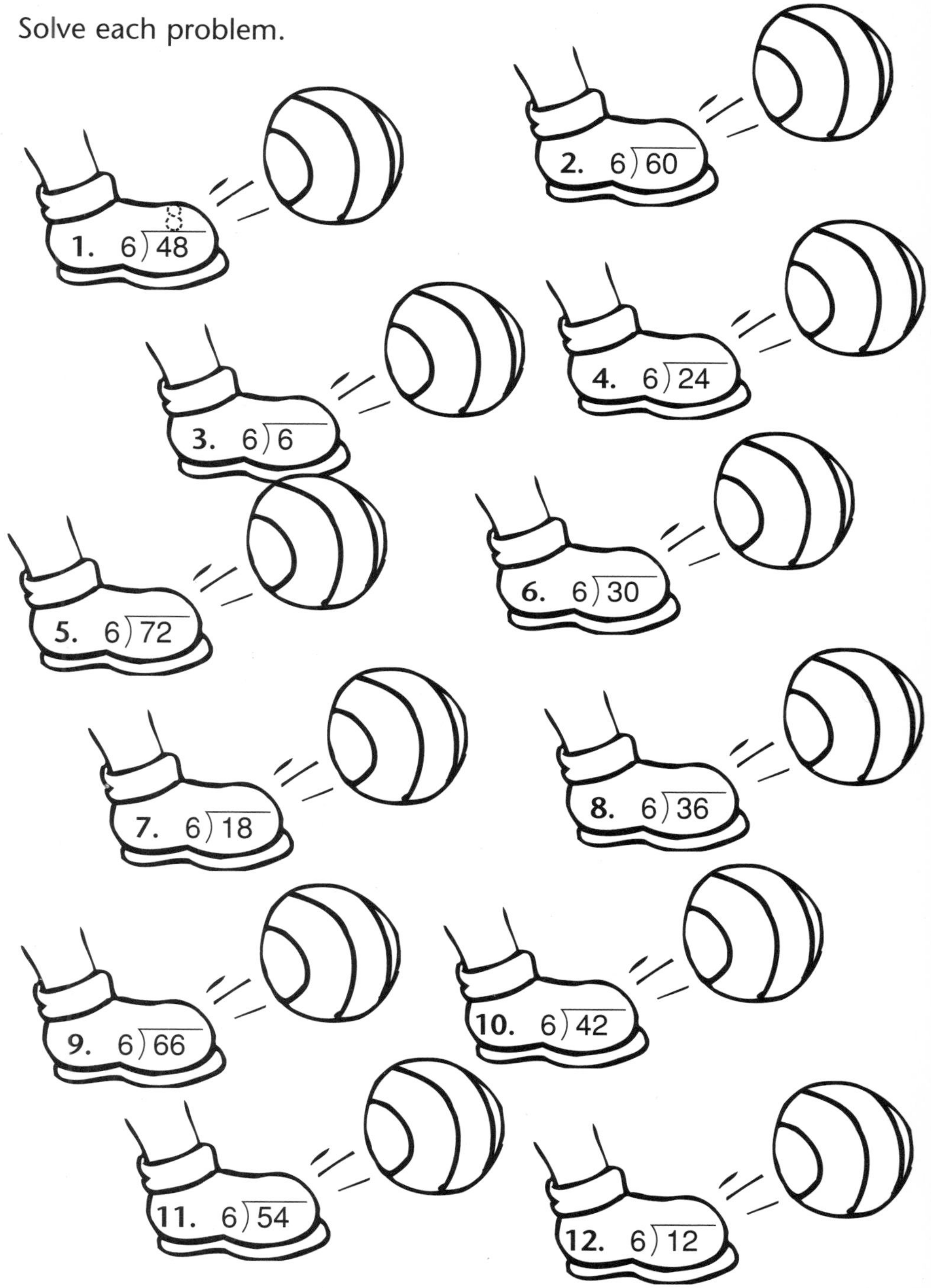

Review Division 1–6

Find each quotient to reach the finish line.

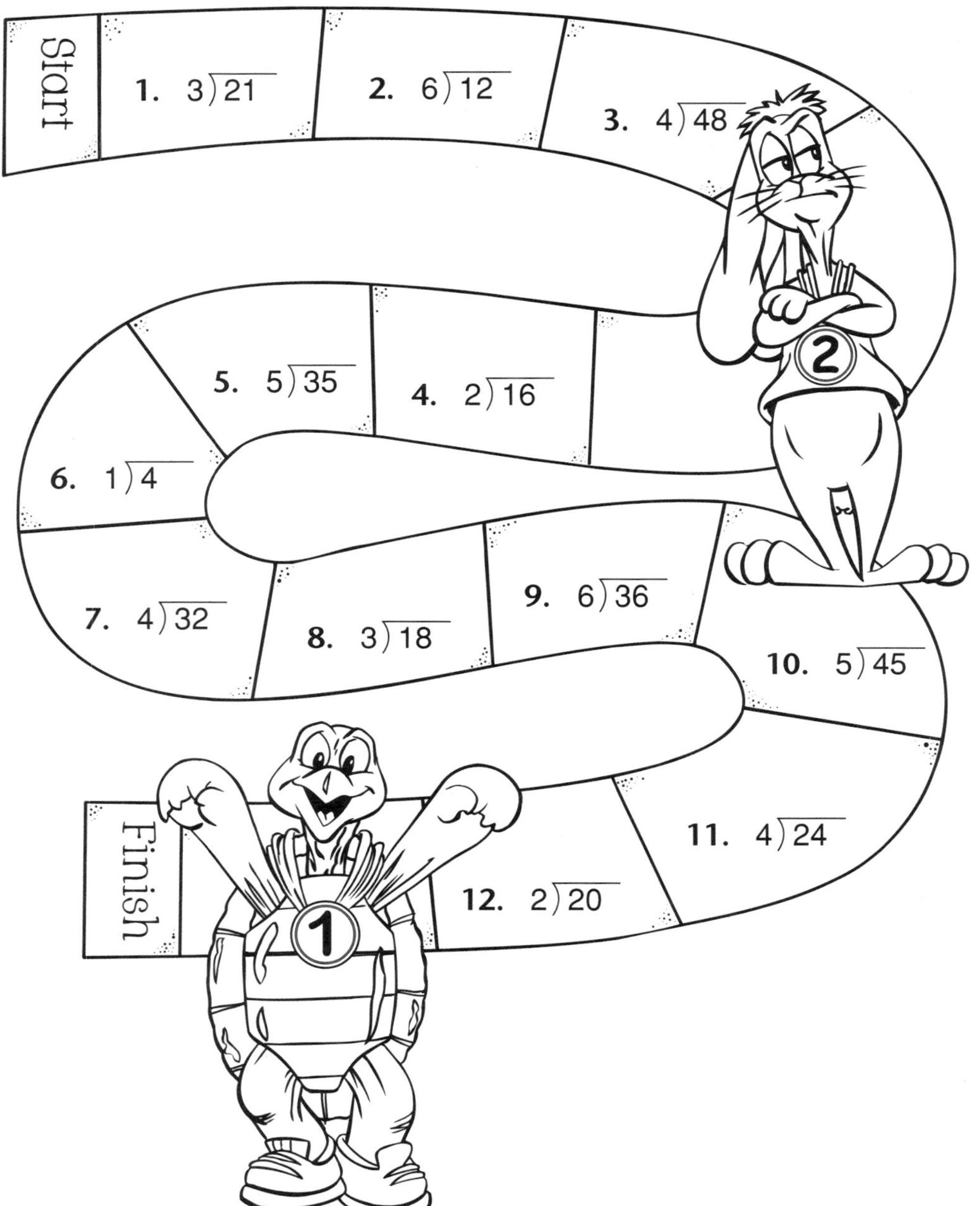

Tic-Tac-Divide

Find each quotient. Draw an **O** over problems with an odd answer. Draw an **X** over problems with even quotients to find the winner of each game.

$2\overline{)12}$	$6\overline{)54}$	$5\overline{)55}$
$6\overline{)36}$	$4\overline{)16}$	$3\overline{)9}$
$5\overline{)35}$	$1\overline{)8}$	$3\overline{)6}$

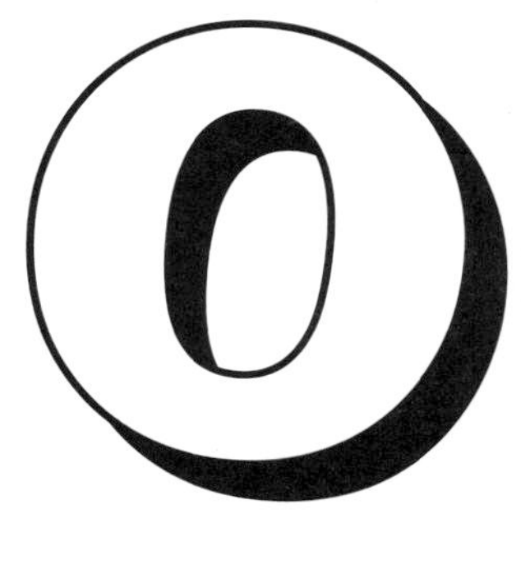

$4\overline{)20}$	$2\overline{)14}$	$6\overline{)18}$
$3\overline{)12}$	$5\overline{)40}$	$5\overline{)45}$
$2\overline{)16}$	$6\overline{)42}$	$4\overline{)24}$

Dividing by 7

Use pictures to help you learn the basic division facts for 7.

1. $\frac{7}{7} =$

2. $\frac{35}{7} =$

3. $\frac{42}{7} =$

4. $\frac{63}{7} =$

5. $\frac{84}{7} =$

6. $\frac{14}{7} =$

7. $\frac{21}{7} =$

8. $\frac{77}{7} =$

9. $\frac{56}{7} =$

10. $\frac{28}{7} =$

11. $\frac{70}{7} =$

12. $\frac{49}{7} =$

Dividing by 7

Send these divisors of 7 up to the heavens.

1. 21 ÷ 7

   3

2. 28 ÷ 7

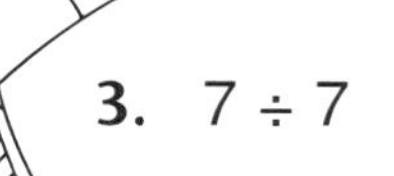

3. 7 ÷ 7

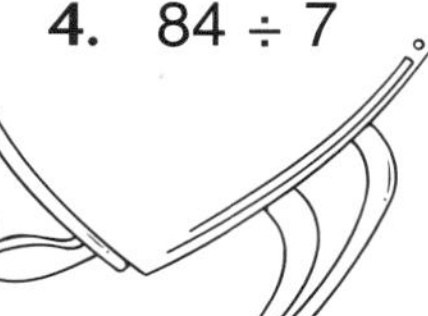

4. 84 ÷ 7

5. 70 ÷ 7

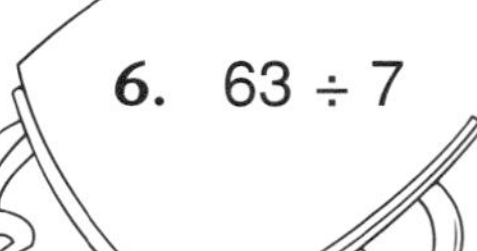

6. 63 ÷ 7

7. 49 ÷ 7

8. 35 ÷ 7

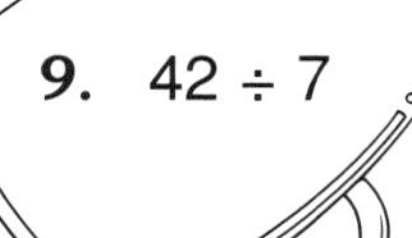

9. 42 ÷ 7

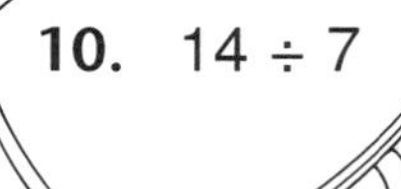

10. 14 ÷ 7

Dividing by 8

Use pictures to help you find each quotient.

1. $24 \div 8 =$ 3

2. $8 \div 8 =$ ______

3. $32 \div 8 =$ ______

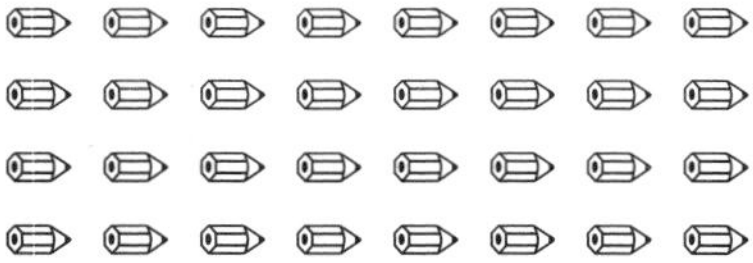

4. $16 \div 8 =$ ______

5. $72 \div 8 =$ ______

6. $80 \div 8 =$ ______

7. $64 \div 8 =$ ______

8. $48 \div 8 =$ ______

9. $40 \div 8 =$ ______

10. $56 \div 8 =$ ______

11. $8 \div 8 =$ ______

12. $96 \div 8 =$ ______

Dividing by 8

Fishing is great for quotients from 8!

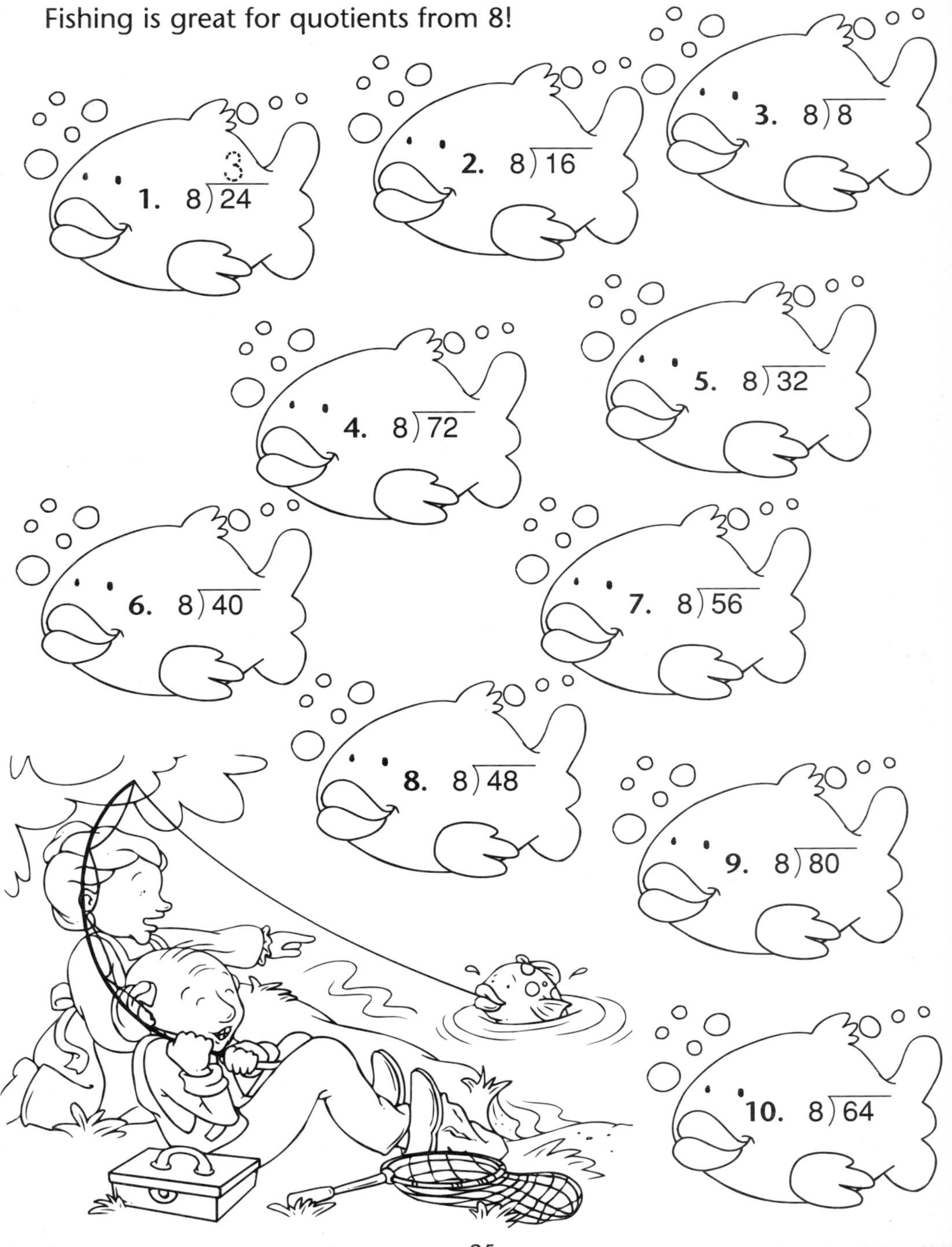

1. 8)24 (sample answer: 3)
2. 8)16
3. 8)8
4. 8)72
5. 8)32
6. 8)40
7. 8)56
8. 8)48
9. 8)80
10. 8)64

Dividing by 9

Draw pictures to help you solve these problems if you need to.

1. $\frac{9}{9} =$

2. $\frac{36}{9} =$

3. $\frac{18}{9} =$

4. $\frac{27}{9} =$

5. $\frac{81}{9} =$

6. $\frac{54}{9} =$

7. $\frac{45}{9} =$

8. $\frac{63}{9} =$

9. $\frac{72}{9} =$

10. $\frac{108}{9} =$

11. $\frac{99}{9} =$

12. $\frac{90}{9} =$

Dividing by 9

Solve the problems on each caboose for Engine No. 9.

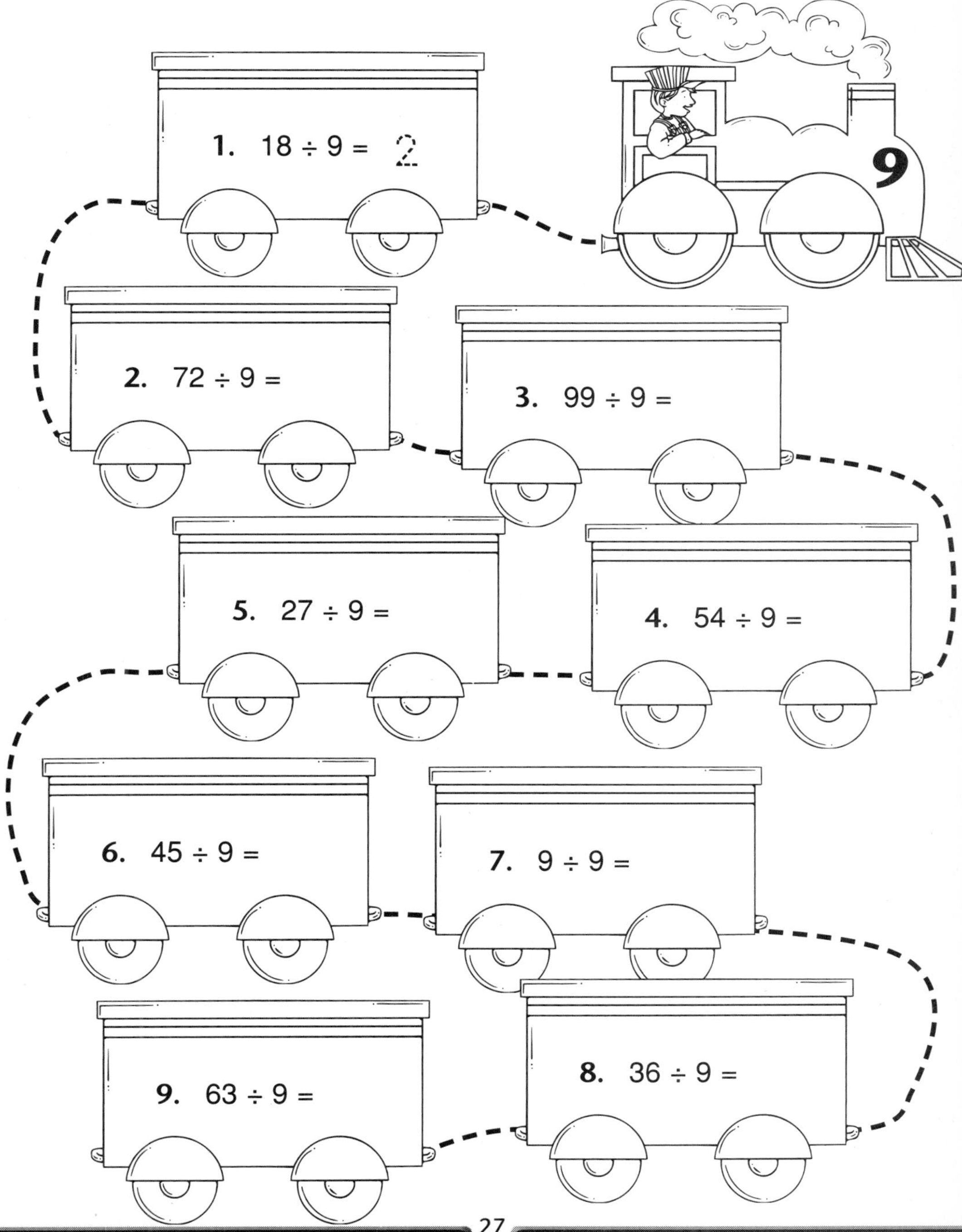

Climbing to the Top

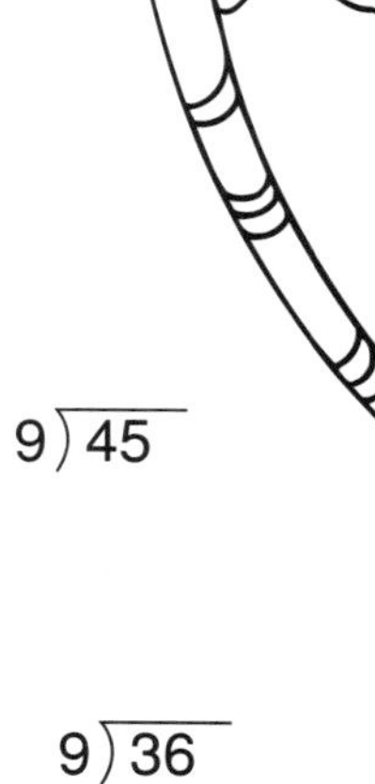

1. $\begin{array}{r} 4 \\ 8\overline{)32} \end{array}$

2. $7\overline{)63}$ $9\overline{)45}$

3. $8\overline{)40}$ $9\overline{)36}$

4. $9\overline{)27}$ 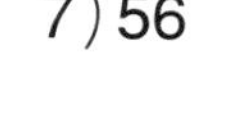 $7\overline{)56}$

5. $7\overline{)21}$ 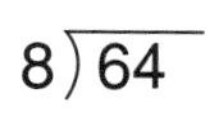 $8\overline{)64}$

6. $8\overline{)16}$ $9\overline{)9}$ $7\overline{)14}$

7. $7\overline{)42}$ $9\overline{)54}$ $8\overline{)24}$

8. $8\overline{)8}$ $7\overline{)49}$ $9\overline{)90}$

Reviewing 7–9

Solve each problem. Draw pictures if you need to.

1. Abby has 32 new flowerpots to sell. She put them in stacks of 8. How many stacks does she make?

   32 ÷ 8 = ______ stacks

2. Mitch is making a "Flower Sale" sign. He will use 7 different paint colors. If he buys all the cans of paint for $49, and each can costs the same, how much did each can cost?

3. Sydney started the day with 27 rosebushes. She arranged them in 9 groups around the store. How many were in each group?

4. Wesley used a forklift to move 72 plants in the store. He could only fit 8 plants at a time on the forklift. How many trips did he make?

Review 1–9 Divisors

Solve each problem, and write the answer in words in the crossword.

Across

1. 42 ÷ 7 = six

2. 30 ÷ 6 =

3. 16 ÷ 8 =

4. 66 ÷ 6 =

5. 12 ÷ 4 =

8. 45 ÷ 5 =

Down

1. 49 ÷ 7 =

2. 36 ÷ 9 =

3. 12 ÷ 1 =

5. 80 ÷ 8 =

6. 24 ÷ 3 =

7. 2 ÷ 2 =

Dividing with 0

If you ever have 0 as the dividend, your answer will always be 0 because you are putting 0 things into whatever group the divisor says.

Example: Putting 0 into groups of 9 still leaves you with 0.

Try a few on your own.

1. $0 \div 6 =$ 0
2. $0 \div 8 =$ ______
3. $0 \div 5 =$ ______
4. $0 \div 2 =$ ______
5. $0 \div 4 =$ ______
6. $0 \div 3 =$ ______

If you ever have 0 in the divisor, it is impossible to do.

Example: You can't put 9 into 0 groups
$9 \div 0 =$ impossible

Try a few on your own.

7. $24 \div 0 =$ impossible
8. $12 \div 0 =$ ______
9. $7 \div 0 =$ ______
10. $36 \div 0 =$ ______

Time Yourself

The basic facts of division 0–9 will help you solve all different kinds of problems in division. Time yourself for one minute on these 20 problems.

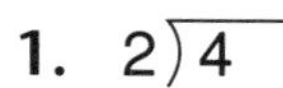

1. 2)4

2. 4)12

3. 7)14

4. 3)15

5. 6)24

6. 4)20

7. 1)3

8. 6)36

9. 3)18

10. 4)24

11. 9)45

12. 8)16

13. 3)9

14. 2)10

15. 7)21

16. 5)25

17. 8)40

18. 9)27

19. 2)12

20. 6)48

Division Patterns

You can use basic facts and patterns to help you divide big numbers.

Example: Basic Facts:

18 ÷ 3 = 6	14 ÷ 2 = 7
180 ÷ 3 = 60	140 ÷ 2 = 70
1,800 ÷ 3 = 600	1,400 ÷ 2 = 700

You simply solve the basic fact and add the zeros found in the dividend onto the quotient.

* Just be careful when there is a zero in the dividend that is part of the basic fact. Don't repeat that zero.

Example: Basic Fact:

20 ÷ 4 = 5
200 ÷ 4 = 50
2,000 ÷ 4 = 500

Try some on your own. Underline the basic fact, and circle the zeros to add on.

1. 12 ÷ 2 = 6
120 ÷ 2 = _______
1,200 ÷ 2 = _______

2. 32 ÷ 8 = _______
320 ÷ 8 = _______
3,200 ÷ 8 = _______

3. 10 ÷ 5 = _______
100 ÷ 5 = _______
1,000 ÷ 5 = _______

4. 90 ÷ 3 = _______
900 ÷ 3 = _______
9,000 ÷ 3 = _______

More Division Patterns

The basic facts and patterns will help you divide in your head. Try to solve these problems mentally. Then check yourself with a calculator.

1. $6 \div 3 =$ _______

$60 \div 3 =$ _______

$600 \div 3 =$ _______

$6{,}000 \div 3 =$ _______

2. $12 \div 6 =$ _______

$120 \div 6 =$ _______

$1{,}200 \div 6 =$ _______

$12{,}000 \div 6 =$ _______

3. $35 \div 5 =$ _______

$350 \div 5 =$ _______

$3{,}500 \div 5 =$ _______

$35{,}000 \div 5 =$ _______

4. $80 \div 4 =$ _______

$800 \div 4 =$ _______

$8{,}000 \div 4 =$ _______

$80{,}000 \div 4 =$ _______

5. $50 \div 5 =$ _______

6. $150 \div 3 =$ _______

7. $1{,}800 \div 9 =$ _______

8. $80 \div 2 =$ _______

9. $200 \div 4 =$ _______

10. $420 \div 6 =$ _______

11. $2{,}700 \div 9 =$ _______

12. $2{,}500 \div 5 =$ _______

Word Problems Using Patterns with 0

Write the problem, and underline the basic fact as you solve each problem.

1. There are 400 students going on a field trip. Each of the 8 teachers will have an equal number of students in a group. How many students will be in each group?

   400 ÷ 8 = ______

2. Miss McKinley's class must watch a movie that is 60 minutes long. She wants to divide the movie into 3 equal periods to watch. How long will each movie-watching period be?

   ______

3. Hayden has 120 movie treats. He wants to put 4 treats together for each classmate. How many classmates does he have?

   ______

4. A field trip bus can hold 80 students. If only 2 students can sit in a seat, how many seats are on the bus?

   ______

Dividing with Remainders

Sometimes when you try to divide a number of objects into groups of equal size, you have some objects left over. The number of objects left over is called the **remainder**.

Example:

$$\begin{array}{r} 5 \\ 4\overline{)20} \\ \underline{-\,20} \\ 0 \end{array}$$

No remainder

$$\begin{array}{r} 5 \text{ r2} \\ 4\overline{)22} \\ \underline{-\,20} \\ 2 \end{array}$$

A remainder

Example:

$4\overline{)6}$

2 hearts are left over

So:

$$\begin{array}{r} 1 \text{ r2} \\ 4\overline{)6} \\ \underline{-\,4} \\ 2 \end{array}$$

Try some on your own.

1. $8\overline{)9}$

2. $3\overline{)8}$

3. $3\overline{)10}$

4. $2\overline{)7}$

5. $5\overline{)9}$

6. $9\overline{)20}$

7. $5\overline{)11}$

8. $6\overline{)14}$

9. $4\overline{)18}$

Basic Facts with Remainders

Try some more basic facts with remainders.

1. $3\overline{)8}$

2. $6\overline{)28}$

3. $5\overline{)18}$

4. $6\overline{)15}$

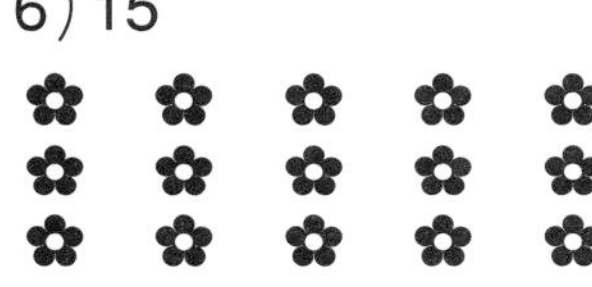

5. $7\overline{)20}$

6. $4\overline{)13}$

7. $6\overline{)27}$

8. $2\overline{)19}$

9. $3\overline{)25}$

10. $4\overline{)9}$

11. $5\overline{)11}$

12. $7\overline{)16}$

More Practice with Basic Facts and Remainders

Draw pictures if you need to.

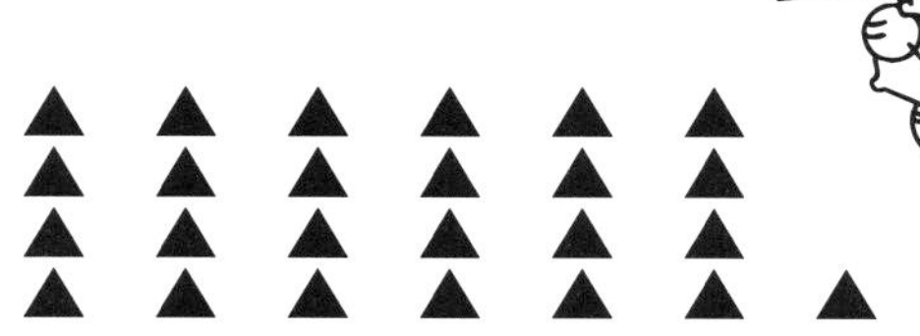

1. 25 ÷ 6 = 4 r1

2. 21 ÷ 4 = ______

3. 6 ÷ 4 = ______

4. 11 ÷ 2 = ______

5. 13 ÷ 3 = ______

6. 22 ÷ 7 = ______

7. 20 ÷ 8 = ______

8. 18 ÷ 5 = ______

Starting Long Division

Instead of using pictures, you can use an **algorithm** to help you solve for the quotient and remainder. An algorithm is a series of steps that help you reach the answer.

Example: $3\overline{)13}$

Step 1
Decide how many times 13 divides into groups of 3. Write that above the 3 in 13.

$$\begin{array}{r} 4 \\ 3\overline{)13} \end{array}$$

Step 2
Multiply 3 x 4, and write that answer under the 13.

$$\begin{array}{r} 4 \\ 3\overline{)13} \\ \underline{12} \end{array}$$

Step 3
Subtract 12 from 13.

$$\begin{array}{r} 4 \\ 3\overline{)13} \\ \underline{-12} \\ 1 \end{array}$$

The quotient is 4 r1.

Try some for practice. Fill in the blanks to complete the algorithm.

1. $\begin{array}{r} 5\overline{)24} \\ \underline{-\ 20} \\ 4 \end{array}$

2. $\begin{array}{r} 2\ r2 \\ 5\overline{)12} \\ \underline{-\quad\ \ } \end{array}$

3. $\begin{array}{r} r \\ 3\overline{)8} \\ \underline{-\ 6} \end{array}$

4. $\begin{array}{r} 7\ r1 \\ 2\overline{)15} \\ \underline{-\quad\ \ } \end{array}$

Division with Remainders

Try your hand at doing simple long division with a remainder.

1. $\begin{array}{r} 7\text{ r1} \\ 3\overline{)22} \\ -\,21 \\ \hline 2 \end{array}$

2. $6\overline{)19}$ − ____

3. $8\overline{)36}$ − ____

4. $4\overline{)23}$ − ____

5. $5\overline{)27}$ − ____

6. $8\overline{)28}$ − ____

7. $7\overline{)52}$ − ____

8. $9\overline{)37}$ − ____

9. $2\overline{)3}$ − ____

10. $3\overline{)29}$ − ____

More Practice

How are you doing remembering your basic facts? It is important to know them so you can concentrate on the algorithm now.

Find each quotient with a remainder.

1. $5\overline{)33}$
$-$ ____

2. $9\overline{)39}$
$-$ ____

3. $7\overline{)52}$
$-$ ____

4. $8\overline{)46}$
$-$ ____

5. $6\overline{)38}$
$-$ ____

6. $7\overline{)59}$
$-$ ____

7. $5\overline{)29}$
$-$ ____

8. $4\overline{)27}$
$-$ ____

9. $8\overline{)66}$
$-$ ____

10. $6\overline{)58}$
$-$ ____

Word Problems with Remainders

1. Hayden was at the amusement park with 12 friends. On one ride, 3 people can ride in a seat. How many friends will have to ride alone?

   13 ÷ 3 = ______

2. The roller coaster scares Gerritt, but he really wants to try it with his mom and dad. The roller coaster seats only hold 2 people. How many will ride alone?

   ______

3. Megan likes to ride the Ferris wheel with her friends. There are 21 friends including Megan. How many seats will they use, and how many will ride alone, if only 2 can sit together?

   ______

4. Addison is in the marching band. The band must form rows with 6 people in each. If there are 55 people in the band, how many complete rows can they form? How many band members will be left?

   ______

Study Page

You have already been doing this with the basic facts of division, but let's take a closer look.

Example: $3\overline{)36}$

Step 1

$3\overline{)36}$

Decide if 3, the divisor, can go into the tens. Yes; 3 can make 1 group.

Step 2

$\begin{array}{r} 1 \\ 3\overline{)36} \end{array}$

Write the 1 above the 3 in the dividend.

Step 3

$\begin{array}{r} 1 \\ 3\overline{)36} \\ \underline{-3} \\ 0 \end{array}$

Multiply 3 x 1, and subtract it from the tens in the dividend.

Step 4

$\begin{array}{r} 1 \\ 3\overline{)36} \\ \underline{-3}\downarrow \\ 06 \end{array}$

Bring down the 6 ones.

Step 5

$\begin{array}{r} 1 \\ 3\overline{)36} \\ \underline{-3} \\ 06 \end{array}$

See if 3, the divisor, can divide into the 6 of the dividend. Yes; it makes 2 groups.

Step 6

$\begin{array}{r} 12 \\ 3\overline{)36} \\ \underline{-3} \\ 06 \end{array}$

Write the 2 above the 6 in the dividend.

Step 7

$\begin{array}{r} 12 \\ 3\overline{)36} \\ \underline{-3} \\ 06 \\ \underline{-6} \\ 0 \end{array}$

Multiply 2 x 3, and subtract it from the ones in the dividend.

You are done because there are no more numbers in the dividend to work with.

Dividing 2-Digit Numbers

Study Page

Let's try some other examples.

Example: $3\overline{)12}$

Step 1

$3\overline{)12}$

Decide if 3, the divisor, can go into the 1. No.

Step 2

$3\overline{)12}$

Decide if 3 can go into 12. Yes; 3 divides 12 into 4 groups.

Step 3

$$\begin{array}{r} 4 \\ 3\overline{)12} \end{array}$$

Write the 4 above the 2 in the dividend.

Step 4

$$\begin{array}{r} 4 \\ 3\overline{)12} \\ \underline{-12} \\ 0 \end{array}$$

Multiply 4x3, and subtract it from 12.

You are done since there are no more numbers to work with.

Example: $4\overline{)68}$

Step 1

$4\overline{)68}$

Decide if 4 can go into the 6 in the dividend. Yes; it makes 1 group.

Step 2

$$\begin{array}{r} 1 \\ 4\overline{)68} \end{array}$$

Write the 1 above the 6.

Step 3

$$\begin{array}{r} 1 \\ 4\overline{)68} \\ \underline{-4} \\ 2 \end{array}$$

Multiply 4 x 1 and subtract it from the 6.

Step 4

$$\begin{array}{r} 1 \\ 4\overline{)68} \\ \underline{-4}\downarrow \\ 28 \end{array}$$

Bring down the 8 ones in the dividend.

Step 5

$$\begin{array}{r} 1 \\ 4\overline{)68} \\ \underline{-4} \\ 28 \end{array}$$

Since 2 is too small for 4 to divide, see how many times 4 goes into 28. It divides 28 into 7 groups.

Step 6

$$\begin{array}{r} 17 \\ 4\overline{)68} \\ \underline{-4} \\ 28 \\ \underline{-28} \\ 0 \end{array}$$

Write the 7 above the 8. Multiply 7 x 4 and subtract the product from 28.

You are done.

Working Up to Long Division

Example:

```
    13
 6)78
  - 6↓
    18
  - 18
     0
```

Solve the following problems.

1. $6\overline{)36}$ — 6; -36; 0

2. $3\overline{)21}$

3. $5\overline{)75}$

4. $4\overline{)64}$

5. $8\overline{)88}$

6. $7\overline{)56}$

7. $4\overline{)48}$

8. $2\overline{)64}$

9. $5\overline{)65}$

10. $3\overline{)51}$

Long division is using multiple math operations, like multiplying, place value, subtracting, and dividing. You write the **algorithm** to show your steps.

More Practice Dividing 2-Digit Numbers

Solve the following problems.

1. $5\overline{)60}$

   −____

   −____

2. $3\overline{)84}$

   −____

   −____

3. $6\overline{)66}$

   −____

   −____

4. $4\overline{)56}$

   −____

   −____

5. $3\overline{)87}$

   −____

   −____

6. $3\overline{)93}$

   −____

   −____

7. $6\overline{)72}$

   −____

   −____

8. $7\overline{)98}$

   −____

   −____

9. $4\overline{)76}$

   −____

   −____

10. $8\overline{)96}$

   −____

   −____

After working out the algorithm, check yourself with a calculator.

Working Onward

Work the problems, and draw a line to the matching quotient.

1. $5\overline{)60}$	**a.** 10
2. $6\overline{)66}$	**b.** 13
3. $3\overline{)39}$	**c.** 11
4. $6\overline{)60}$	**d.** 12
5. $4\overline{)76}$	**e.** 32
6. $3\overline{)96}$	**f.** 19

Dividing 2-Digit Numbers with a Remainder

Study Page

Example: $4\overline{)93}$

Steps 1 and 2

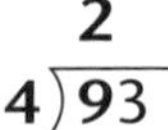

$$\begin{array}{r} \mathbf{2} \\ \mathbf{4\overline{)93}} \end{array}$$

Decide if 4 can go into 9. Yes; it can make 2 groups. Write the 2 above the 9 in the dividend.

Steps 3 and 4

$$\begin{array}{r} \mathbf{2} \\ \mathbf{4\overline{)93}} \\ \underline{\mathbf{-\,8}\downarrow} \\ \mathbf{13} \end{array}$$

Multiply 4 x 2 and subtract it from the tens in the dividend. Bring down the 3 to make a new dividend of 13.

Steps 5, 6, and 7

$$\begin{array}{r} 23 \\ 4\overline{)93} \\ \underline{-\,8} \\ 13 \\ \underline{\mathbf{-\,12}} \\ 1 \end{array}$$

See how many times 4 goes into 13. It goes into 13 three times. Write 3 above the 3 in the dividend. Multiply 4 x 3, and subtract the answer from 13.

Step 8

$$\begin{array}{r} \mathbf{23\ r1} \\ 4\overline{)93} \\ \underline{-\,8} \\ 13 \\ \underline{-\,12} \\ \mathbf{1} \end{array}$$

Since there are no more numbers in the dividend to bring down, and the number left over (1) is smaller than the divisor, you have a remainder.

Dividing 2-Digit Numbers with a Remainder

Work the following problems.

1. $\begin{array}{r} 3\square \text{ r1} \\ 2\overline{)75} \\ -\ 6\downarrow \\ 1\square \\ -\square\square \\ \square \end{array}$

2. $\begin{array}{r} \square\square \text{ r}\square \\ 4\overline{)89} \\ -\ 8\downarrow \\ 0\square \\ -\ \square \\ \square \end{array}$

3. $6\overline{)92}$

4. $7\overline{)85}$

5. $3\overline{)73}$

6. $4\overline{)65}$

7. $3\overline{)35}$

8. $6\overline{)76}$

9. $2\overline{)53}$

10. $3\overline{)44}$

More Practice

Solve for the quotient with a remainder.

1. $5\overline{)82}$ (quotient □□ r □; $-$□, □2, $-$□□, □)

2. $9\overline{)84}$

3. $3\overline{)67}$

4. $4\overline{)99}$

5. $6\overline{)87}$

6. $7\overline{)89}$

7. $3\overline{)83}$

8. $2\overline{)65}$

9. $8\overline{)99}$

10. $6\overline{)69}$

Use either the remainder or the quotient to help you answer these story problems.

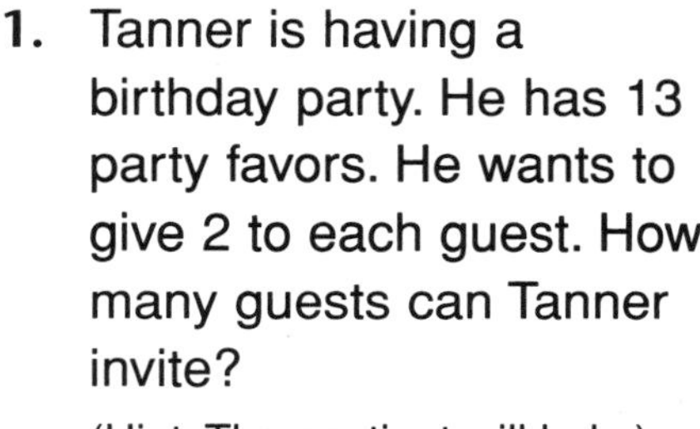

1. Tanner is having a birthday party. He has 13 party favors. He wants to give 2 to each guest. How many guests can Tanner invite?
(Hint: The quotient will help.)

2. Max brought balloons for everybody at the birthday party. He bought 10 balloons. How many balloons will be left over if 7 people are at the party?
(Hint: Use the remainder.)

3. Kemry loves birthday cake. She wants to share the cake equally with 6 guests and herself. There are 19 pieces of cake cut. How many pieces will each person get?
(Hint: $19 \div 7$)

4. Quincey received a small bag of jellybeans as a gift. There are 83 jellybeans in the bag. He wants to share them equally among 7 people. How many will each person get?

Dividing a 1-Digit Number into a 3-Digit Number

With a 3-digit number, you must bring down one more number in the dividend to complete the problem.

Example:

$$\begin{array}{r} 213 \\ 3\overline{)639} \\ -6\downarrow \\ \hline 03 \\ -3\downarrow \\ \hline 09 \\ -9 \\ \hline 0 \end{array}$$

Try these. They do not have remainders.

1. $\begin{array}{r} 14\square \\ 2\overline{)284} \\ -2\downarrow \\ \hline 08 \\ -8\downarrow \\ \hline 04 \\ -\square \\ \hline \square \end{array}$

2. $\begin{array}{r} \square 37 \\ 4\overline{)948} \\ -8\downarrow \\ \hline 1\square \\ -12\downarrow \\ \hline 02\square \\ -\square\square \\ \hline \square\square \end{array}$

3. $5\overline{)555}$

4. $3\overline{)936}$

5. $2\overline{)526}$

6. $3\overline{)741}$

Dividing 3-Digit Numbers by 1 Digit with No Remainder

Sometimes you must solve a problem by looking at the first two digits, dividing the divisor into them, and then bringing down the third digit to complete the problem.

Example:

```
   64
8)512
 -48↓
   32
  -32
    0
```

First divide 51 by 8 since 5 is too small to divide by 8.

Then bring down the 2 to make 32.

Try solving a few like the sample.
Use a calculator to check your work.

1.

```
   4□
7)336
 -□□↓
   56
 - □□
    □
```

2.

```
   □□
4)228
 -□□↓
   2□
  -□□
    0
```

3. 9)747

−

−

4. 6)210

−

−

5. 5)285

−

−

6. 8)768

−

−

Dividing 3-Digit Numbers by 1 Digit with a Remainder

Keep following the same long division steps, but at the end, make sure your remainder is smaller than the divisor.

Example:

```
   175 r1
3)526
 - 3
   22
 - 21
   16
 - 15
    1
```

Solve for the quotients.

1. $2\overline{)357}$

2. $4\overline{)975}$

3. $5\overline{)823}$

4. $5\overline{)348}$

5. $7\overline{)439}$

6. $8\overline{)591}$

More Practice with 3-Digit Numbers

Match each problem to its quotient. Some may have a remainder; others may not.

1. $4\overline{)918}$ **a.** 109 r8

2. $4\overline{)228}$ **b.** 123 r3

3. $5\overline{)378}$ **c.** 57

4. $9\overline{)989}$ **d.** 137

5. $6\overline{)822}$ **e.** 75 r3

6. $8\overline{)987}$ **f.** 229 r2

Zeros in the Quotient

Sometimes there may not be enough tens or ones to divide into. If so, write 0 in the quotient over the proper number in the dividend. Then continue with the remaining steps to finish solving the problem.

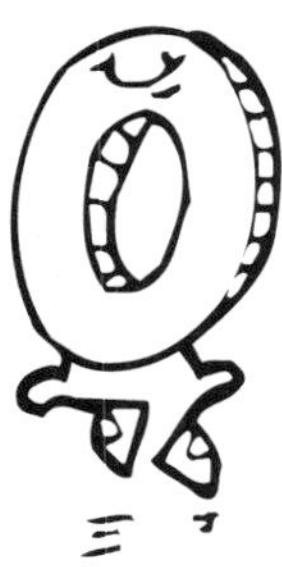

Example:

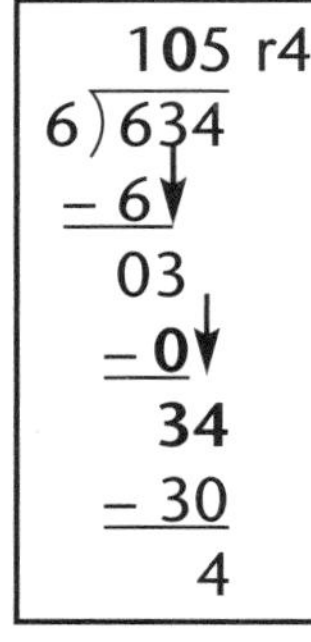

```
   105 r4
6)634
 - 6
   03
  - 0
   34
  - 30
     4
```

3 is too small to divide by 6, so you put a 0 in the quotient, multiply, and subtract it.

Fill in the blanks to solve these problems.

1.
```
   1□□ r□
4)417
 - 4
   01
 -  □
   17
 - □□
    □
```

2.
```
   □□□ r□
5)754
 - 5
   25
 - □□
   04
 -  □
    □
```

3. $2\overline{)61}$

4. $6\overline{)624}$

More Practice with 0's in the Quotient

Solve the problems.

1. $2\overline{)415}$

2. $5\overline{)363}$

3. $3\overline{)541}$

4. $8\overline{)861}$

5. $9\overline{)92}$

6. $8\overline{)324}$

Story Problems with 0 in the Quotient

1. There were 455 people sitting on benches at the cow show. If 9 people sat on each bench, how many benches did they need?

2. Breanna is giving away peaches at the county fair. She brought 325 peaches. How many people could each get 3 free peaches? How many peaches would Kelly have left?

3. Megan has a booth where people can make bead necklaces. If she puts out 240 beads at a time, how many necklaces can be made if 8 beads fit on a string?

4. There are 818 rabbits shown at the fair. If there are 9 cages in a row and one rabbit in each cage, how many full rows of rabbits are there to see?

Dividing Money

Divide money the same as you would whole numbers. Write the dollar sign and the decimal point in the quotient.

Example:

Divide 768 by 3	Divide $7.68 by 3
$\begin{array}{r} 256 \\ 3\overline{)768} \\ -6\downarrow \\ 16 \\ -15\downarrow \\ 18 \\ -18 \\ 0 \end{array}$	$\begin{array}{r} \$2.56 \\ 3\overline{)\$7.68} \\ -6\downarrow \\ 16 \\ -15\downarrow \\ 18 \\ -18 \\ 0 \end{array}$

1. $5\overline{)\$6.15}$

2. $2\overline{)\$7.76}$

3. $7\overline{)\$8.05}$

4. $4\overline{)\$7.44}$

Dividing Money

Sometimes the divisor leaves you with cents instead of dollars, so you must put a 0 in the quotient before the decimal point.

Example:

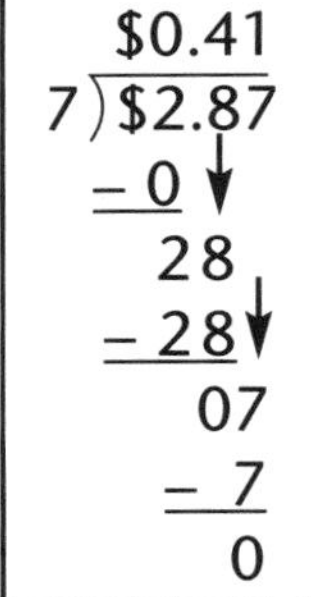

Match each problem with its answer.

1. $5\overline{)\$4.20}$ **a.** \$0.70

2. $6\overline{)\$6.72}$ **b.** \$0.23

3. $3\overline{)\$2.10}$ **c.** \$0.84

4. $4\overline{)\$0.92}$ **d.** \$1.12

Basic Facts for Dividing by 10

The basic facts will help you start to divide 2-digit numbers into larger numbers.

The zeros help to cancel each other out, so just look at the digit in the tens place.

Example: $10\overline{)90}$

$$\begin{array}{r} 9 \\ 10\overline{)90} \\ \underline{-\,90} \\ 0 \end{array}$$

Think: 9 ÷ 1 = 9
Place the 9 above the 0, multiply, and subtract.

Try dividing 10 into the following dividends.

1. $10\overline{)80}$

2. $10\overline{)70}$

3. $10\overline{)20}$

4. $10\overline{)50}$

5. $10\overline{)60}$

6. $10\overline{)10}$

Basic Facts for Multiples of 10

These problems work similarly to dividing by 10. You can cancel the zero and focus on a basic fact.

Example: $30\overline{)60}$

$$\begin{array}{r} 2 \\ 30\overline{)60} \\ -\underline{60} \\ 0 \end{array}$$

Think: $6 \div 3 = 2$
Place the 2 above the 0, multiply, and subtract.

These problems can usually be worked mentally instead of writing the whole algorithm.

Try doing these problems mentally. Then check yourself with a calculator.

1. $40\overline{)80}$

2. $30\overline{)90}$

3. $20\overline{)40}$

4. $40\overline{)40}$

5. $10\overline{)60}$

6. $20\overline{)80}$

Dividing by Multiples of 10

Try dividing these problems using either mental math or the algorithm to help you find the quotient. They will have a remainder.

Example:

$$\begin{array}{r} 3 \text{ r}2 \\ 20\overline{)62} \\ -\underline{60} \\ 2 \end{array} \qquad \begin{array}{r} 1 \text{ r}22 \\ 50\overline{)72} \\ -\underline{50} \\ 22 \end{array}$$

1. $40\overline{)48}$

2. $20\overline{)82}$

3. $10\overline{)76}$

4. $30\overline{)99}$

5. $50\overline{)72}$

6. $90\overline{)95}$

Basic Facts for Dividing by 11

The basic facts for dividing by 11 can also be done mentally if you just think of the first digit in both the divisor and the dividend.

Example: $11\overline{)44}$

$$\begin{array}{r} 4 \\ 11\overline{)44} \\ \underline{-44} \\ 0 \end{array}$$

Think: 4 ÷ 1 = 4
Write the 4 above the ones digit in the dividend.

1. $11\overline{)66}$

2. $11\overline{)22}$

3. $11\overline{)99}$

4. $11\overline{)77}$

5. $11\overline{)33}$

6. $11\overline{)88}$

7. $11\overline{)44}$

8. $11\overline{)55}$

Dividing by 11 with Remainders

When 11 doesn't go into the number exactly, think of the basic fact that is closest to the dividend you are asked to solve for.

Example: $11\overline{)46}$

$$\begin{array}{r} 4\text{ r}2 \\ 11\overline{)46} \\ -44 \\ \hline 2 \end{array}$$

Think: 44 is close to 46. So 44 ÷ 11 = 4 plus a remainder. Multiply by 4, and subtract to get a remainder of 2.

Try solving for the basic fact, and complete the algorithm to get the remainder.

1. $11\overline{)35}$

2. $11\overline{)90}$

3. $11\overline{)25}$

4. $11\overline{)48}$

5. $11\overline{)78}$

6. $11\overline{)15}$

Basic Facts for Dividing by 12

Figure out how many 12's will divide into each of the following dividends.

1. $12\overline{)24}$

2. $12\overline{)96}$

3. $12\overline{)60}$

4. $12\overline{)108}$

5. $12\overline{)120}$

6. $12\overline{)48}$

7. $12\overline{)84}$

8. $12\overline{)36}$

9. $12\overline{)72}$

10. $12\overline{)144}$

11. $12\overline{)132}$

12. $12\overline{)12}$

Make the Score

Critical Thinking Skills

Rearrange the numbers on the balls to create a dividend and a divisor that will match the quotient.

1. <u>49</u> ÷ <u>7</u> = 7

2. ____ ÷ ____ = 2

3. ____ ÷ ____ = 3

4. ____ ÷ ____ = 8

5. ____ ÷ ____ = 9

6. ____ ÷ ____ = 5

7. ____ ÷ ____ = 9

8. ____ ÷ ____ = 6

274

9. ____ ÷ ____ = 6

Critical Thinking Skills

Climbing to the Top

Start at the bottom of the stairs. Find the quotient for the first problem, and then use it as the divisor for the next step. Repeat until you reach the top.

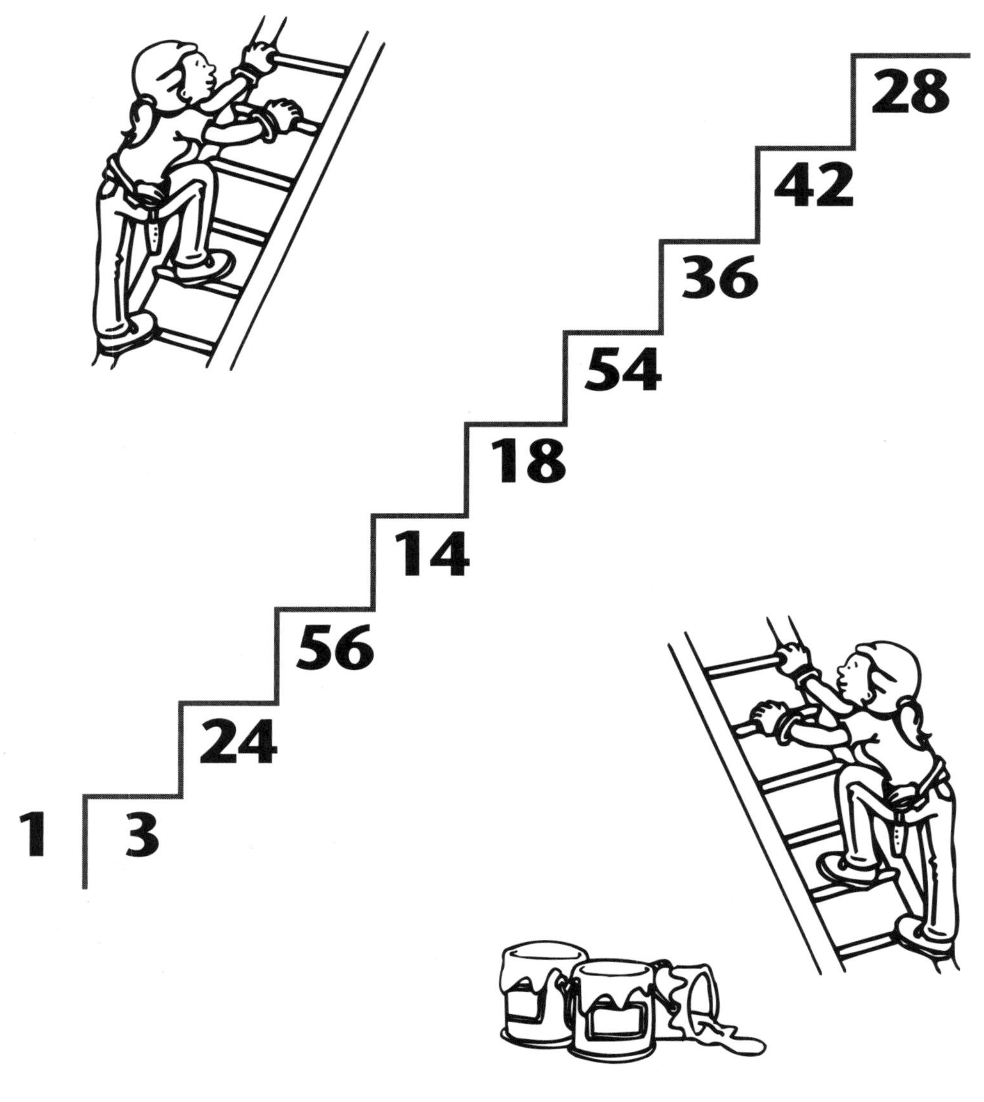

Measuring Your Division Skills

Critical Thinking Skills

Use what you know about measurements and division to help make the equivalents. If you are unsure of what the equivalents should be, use a dictionary to help you.

1. 36 inches = ___3___ feet

   Hint: 12 inches = 1 foot.
   So, 36 ÷ 12 = 3 feet.

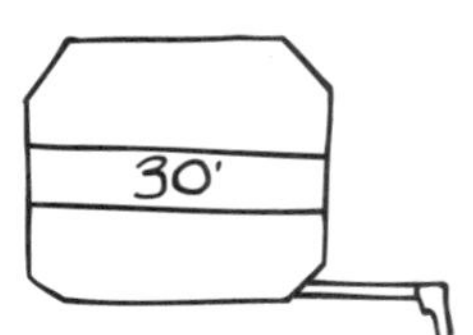

2. 16 fluid ounces = ________ cups

3. ________ gallons = 8 quarts

4. 72 feet = ________ yards

5. 48 ounces = ________ pounds

6. ________ pints = 4 cups

7. 4 pints = ________ quarts

Critical Thinking Skills

Timing Up Division

1. Mrs. Breur's class is 60 minutes long. She wants to divide her class time into 3 equal sections. How long will each section be?

____

2. For his math test, Zach must figure out how many days there are in 72 hours. What would the correct answer be?

____

3. Grant's science experiment on decomposition says it takes 730 days to complete. How many years is that?

____

4. McKinley will be in third grade in 48 months. How many years will it be until she is a third grader?

____

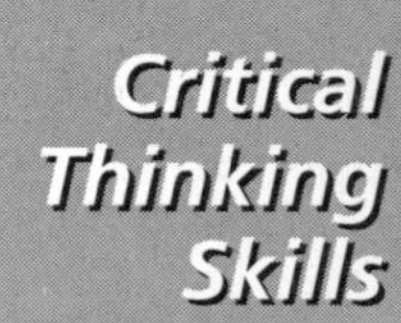

Cooking Up Division

The recipe Lori is using is too big for her party. She wants to only make a **third** of the recipe. Help her change the recipe so she doesn't make too much. (Hint: Use division.)

Triple Chocolate Cookies Recipe

Recipe	1/3 of Recipe
3 cups of butter	**1 cup of butter**
6 cups of sugar	____________
$\frac{3}{4}$ teaspoon of salt	____________
24 tablespoons of cocoa	____________
9 eggs	____________
6 teaspoons of vanilla	____________
3 teaspoons of baking soda	____________
6 cups of flour	____________

Critical Thinking Skills

Tic-Tac-Toe Division

Test your knowledge on odd and even numbers to find who wins the game. Put an **O** on the odd answers. Put an **X** on the even answers.

$5\overline{)10}$	$4\overline{)8}$	$24 \div 4$
$4\overline{)36}$	$35 \div 5$	$4\overline{)32}$
$45 \div 5$	$5\overline{)30}$	$12 \div 4$

$28 \div 4$	$5\overline{)30}$	$45 \div 5$
$4\overline{)16}$	$32 \div 4$	$5\overline{)15}$
$20 \div 4$	$12 \div 3$	$4\overline{)8}$

$5\overline{)25}$	$8 \div 4$	$4\overline{)16}$
$32 \div 4$	$5\overline{)20}$	$5\overline{)35}$
$5\overline{)40}$	$4\overline{)12}$	$15 \div 5$

$36 \div 12$	$9\overline{)18}$	$7\overline{)42}$
$2\overline{)12}$	$45 \div 9$	$64 \div 8$
$9\overline{)81}$	$24 \div 6$	$7\overline{)49}$

Division Riddles

Critical Thinking Skills

1. What is my quotient?
   My number is 63. I like to be divided by an odd number. My divisor is the answer to 14 ÷ 2. What is my quotient?

   ____

Knock, knock!

Who's there?

Orange!

Orange who?

Orange you glad you heard this joke?!

2. What is my divisor?
   My quotient is 162. But my dividend is twice as many. I am used a lot when problems ask for a half. My whole problem is full of even numbers, so what is my divisor?

   ____

3. What is my dividend?
   I am an odd, 2-digit number. If you add my divisor and my quotient together, you will get the numeral 14. You might even think my divisor and quotient are twins. If you add the 2 digits in my dividend, you will get 13. What is my dividend?

   ____

Critical Thinking Skills

Just above Average Division

You find an average by dividing the **sum** of a group numbers by the number of **addends**.

For example, to find the average of 2, 4, and 6, add 2 + 4 + 6 = 12. There are 3 numbers (2, 4, and 6), so divide 12 by 3, which equals 4. That's the average.

Find the averages. Match each problem with its answer.

1. 21 + 34 + 44 =	**a.** 96
2. 278 + 246 =	**b.** 67
3. 85 + 100 + 100 + 100 + 95 =	**c.** 190
4. 4 + 6 + 7 + 12 + 11 =	**d.** 33
5. 125 + 248 + 214 + 173 =	**e.** 8
6. 81 + 57 + 63 =	**f.** 262

Answer Pages

Page 4

1. quotient
2. dividend
3. quotient
4. divisor
5. dividend
6. divisor
7. dividend
8. quotient

Page 5

1. 6
2. 9
3. 5
4. 4
5. 2
6. 3
7. 4
8. 3

Page 6

1. 4
2. 6
3. 1
4. 3
5. 2
6. 5
7. 2
8. 3

Page 7

1. 2
2. 11
3. 6
4. 8
5. 5
6. 10
7. 3
8. 7
9. 9
10. 4
11. 12

Page 8

1. 3
2. 2
3. 5
4. 8
5. 1
6. 6
7. 7
8. 4
9. 9
10. 10

Page 9

1. 12
2. 1
3. 4
4. 7
5. 3
6. 9

1. 1
2. 6
3. 12
4. 3
5. 11

1. 5
2. 10
3. 6
4. 2
5. 7
6. 9

Page 10

1. 6
2. 2
3. 5
4. 3
5. 1
6. 4
7. 10
8. 7

Page 11

1. 1
2. 4
3. 7
4. 5
5. 3

1. 3
2. 6
3. 9
4. 2
5. 10

1. 2
2. 5
3. 8
4. 4
5. 1

Page 12

1. C
2. E
3. D
4. A
5. B
6. 4
7. 4
8. 4
9. 6
10. 6

Page 13

1. 6 animals
2. 3 cards
3. 5 kittens
4. 7 rabbits

Page 14

1. 1　　2. 3
3. 6　　4. 5
5. 2　　6. 8
7. 4　　8. 11
9. 7　　10. 9
11. 10　　12. 12

Page 15

1. 3	9	1	5
2. 2	11	7	4
3. 6	1	9	8
4. 10	12	3	2

Page 16

1. 1　　2. 6
3. 4　　4. 2
5. 7　　6. 9
7. 11　　8. 12
9. 3　　10. 5

Page 17

1. 4
2. 12　　3. 6
4. 4　　5. 5
6. 9　　7. 7
8. 1　　9. 8
10. 2　　11. 10
12. 3　　13. 11

Page 18

1. 1　　2. 6
3. 8　　4. 3
5. 5　　6. 10
7. 11　　8. 2
9. 4　　10. 9
11. 7　　12. 12

Page 19

1. 8　　2. 10
3. 1　　4. 4
5. 12　　6. 5
7. 3　　8. 6
9. 11　　10. 7
11. 9　　12. 2

Page 20

1. 7　　2. 2
3. 12　　4. 8
5. 7　　6. 4
7. 8　　8. 6
9. 6　　10. 9
11. 6　　12. 10

Page 21

X 2)12 = 6	O 6)54 = 9	O 5)55 = 11	O 4)20 = 5	O 2)14 = 7	O 6)18 = 3
X 6)36 = 6	X 4)16 = 4	O 3)9 = 3	X 3)12 = 4	X 5)40 = 8	O 5)45 = 9
O 5)35 = 7	X 1)8 = 8	X 3)6 = 2	X 2)16 = 8	O 6)42 = 7	X 4)24 = 6

Page 22

1. 1　　2. 5
3. 6　　4. 9
5. 12　　6. 2
7. 3　　8. 11
9. 8　　10. 4
11. 10　　12. 7

Page 23

1. 3　　2. 4
3. 1　　4. 12
5. 10　　6. 9
7. 7　　8. 5
9. 6　　10. 2

Page 24

1. 3　　2. 1
3. 4　　4. 2
5. 9　　6. 10
7. 8　　8. 6
9. 5　　10. 7
11. 1　　12. 12

Page 25

1. 3　　2. 2
3. 1　　4. 9
5. 4　　6. 5
7. 7　　8. 6
9. 10　　10. 8

Page 26

1. 1   2. 4
3. 2   4. 3
5. 9   6. 6
7. 5   8. 7
9. 8   10. 12
11. 11   12. 10

Page 27

1. 2
2. 8   3. 11
4. 6   5. 3
6. 5   7. 1
9. 7   8. 4

Page 28

1. 4
2. 9   5
3. 5   4
4. 3   8
5. 3   8
6. 2   1   2
7. 6   6   3
8. 1   7   10

Page 29

1. 4 stacks   2. 7 dollars
3. 3 bushes   4. 9 trips

Page 30

Across	Down
1. six	1. seven
2. five	2. four
3. two	3. twelve
4. eleven	5. ten
5. three	6. eight
8. nine	7. one

										1 s	i	x			
							2 f	i	v	e					
					3 t	w	o			v					
					w		u			4 e	l	e	v	e	n
					e		r			n					
					l										
					v										
		5 t	h	r	e	6 e									
7 o		e				i									
8 n	i	n	e			g									
e						h									
						t									

Page 31

1. 0   2. 0
3. 0   4. 0
5. 0   6. 0

7. impossible   8. impossible
9. impossible   10. impossible

Page 32

1. 2   2. 3
3. 2   4. 5
5. 4   6. 5
7. 3   8. 6
9. 6   10. 6
11. 5   12. 2
13. 3   14. 5
15. 3   16. 5
17. 5   18. 3
19. 6   20. 8

Page 33

1. 6, 60, 600, (<u>12</u>)   2. 4, 40, 400, (<u>32</u>)

3. 2, 20, 200, (<u>10</u>)   4. 30, 300, 3000, (<u>90</u>)

Page 34

1. 2, 20, 200, 2000   2. 2, 20, 200, 2000

3. 7, 70, 700, 7000   4. 20, 200, 2000, 20,000

5. 10   6. 50
7. 200   8. 40
9. 50   10. 70
11. 300   12. 500

Page 35

1. 50 students
2. 20 minutes
3. 30 classmates
4. 40 seats

Page 36

1. 1 r1 2. 2 r2
3. 3 r1 4. 3 r1
5. 1 r4 6. 2 r2
7. 2 r1 8. 2 r2
9. 4 r2

Page 37

1. 2 r2 2. 4 r4
3. 3 r3 4. 2 r3
5. 2 r6 6. 3 r1
7. 4 r3 8. 9 r1
9. 8 r1 10. 2 r1
11. 2 r1 12. 2 r2

Page 38

1. 4 r1
2. 5 r1
3. 1 r2
4. 5 r1
5. 4 r1
6. 3 r1
7. 2 r4
8. 3 r3

Page 39

1. $\begin{array}{r} \textbf{4r4} \\ 5\overline{)24} \\ \underline{-20} \\ 4 \end{array}$ 2. $\begin{array}{r} 2r2 \\ 5\overline{)12} \\ \underline{-\textbf{10}} \\ \textbf{2} \end{array}$

3. $\begin{array}{r} \textbf{2r2} \\ 3\overline{)8} \\ \underline{-6} \\ \textbf{2} \end{array}$ 4. $\begin{array}{r} 7r1 \\ 2\overline{)15} \\ \underline{\textbf{-14}} \\ \textbf{1} \end{array}$

Page 40

1. 7 r1 2. 3 r1
3. 4 r4 4. 5 r3
5. 5 r2 6. 3 r4
7. 7 r3 8. 4 r1
9. 1 r1 10. 9 r2

Page 41

1. 6 r3 2. 4 r3
3. 7 r3 4. 5 r6
5. 6 r2 6. 8 r3
7. 5 r4 8. 6 r3
9. 8 r2 10. 9 r4

Page 42

1. 1 friend
2. 1 person
3. 11 seats; 1 alone
4. 9 rows; 1 band member left

Page 45

1. 6 2. 7
3. 15 4. 16
5. 11 6. 8
7. 12 8. 32
9. 13 10. 17

Page 46

1. 12 2. 28
3. 11 4. 14
5. 29 6. 31
7. 12 8. 14
9. 19 10. 12

Page 47

1. D
2. C
3. B
4. A
5. F
6. E

Page 49

1. $2\overline{)75}$ = 37r1; -6; 15; -14; 1
2. $4\overline{)89}$ = 22r1; -8; 09; -8; 1
3. 15 r2
4. 12 r1
5. 24 r1
6. 16 r1
7 11 r2
8. 12 r4
9. 26 r1
10. 14 r2

Page 50

1. 16 r2
2. 9 r3
3. 22 r1
4. 24 r3
5. 14 r3
6. 12 r5
7. 27 r2
8. 32 r1
9. 12 r3
10. 11 r3

Page 51

1. 6 guests
2. 3 balloons left
3. 2 pieces
4. 11 jelly beans

Page 52

1. 142
2. 237
3. 111
4. 312
5. 263
6. 247

Page 53

1. 48
2. 57
3. 83
4. 35
5. 57
6. 96

Page 54

1. 178 r1
2. 243 r3
3. 164 r3
4. 69 r3
5. 62 r5
6. 73 r7

Page 55

1. F
2. C
3. E
4. A
5. D
6. B

Page 56

1. 104 r1
2. 150 r4
3. 30 r1
4. 104

Page 57

1. 207 r1
2. 72 r3
3. 180 r1
4. 107 r5
5. 10 r2
6. 40 r4

Page 58

1. 51 benches
2. 108 people; 1 peach left over
3. 30 necklaces
4. 90 full rows

Page 59

1. $1.23
2. $ 3.88
3. $1.15
4. $1.86

Page 60

1. C
2. D
3. A
4. B

Page 61

1. 8
2. 7
3. 2
4. 5
5. 6
6. 1

Page 62

1. 2
2. 3
3. 2
4. 1
5. 6
6. 4

Page 63

1. 1 r8
2. 4 r2
3. 7 r6
4. 3 r9
5. 1 r22
6. 1 r5

Page 64

1. 6
2. 2
3. 9
4. 7
5. 3
6. 8
7. 4
8. 5

Page 65

1. 3 r2
2. 8 r2
3. 2 r3
4. 4 r4
5. 7 r1
6. 1 r4

Page 66

1. 2
2. 8
3. 5
4. 9
5. 10
6. 4
7. 7
8. 3
9. 6
10. 12
11. 11
12. 1

Page 67

1. 49 ÷ 7
2. 18 ÷ 9
3. 27 ÷ 9
4. 32 ÷ 4 or 24 ÷ 3
5. 45 ÷ 5
6. 40 ÷ 8
7. 63 ÷ 7
8. 36 ÷ 6
9. 42 ÷ 7

Page 68

4
7 | 28
6 | 42
6 | 36
9 | 54
2 | 18
7 | 14
8 | 56
3 | 24
1 | 3

Page 69

1. 3 feet
2. 2 cups
3. 2 gallons
4. 24 yards
5. 3 pounds
6. 2 pints
7. 2 quarts

Page 70

1. 20 minutes
2. 3 days
3. 2 years
4. 4 years

Page 71

1 cup butter
2 cups sugar
$\frac{1}{4}$ teaspoon of salt
8 tablespoons of cocoa
3 eggs
2 teaspoons of vanilla
1 teaspoon of baking soda
2 cups of flour

Page 72

X: 5)10 = 2	X: 4)8 = 2	X: 24 ÷ 4 = 6
O: 4)36 = 9	O: 35 ÷ 5 = 7	X: 4)32 = 8
O: 45 ÷ 5 = 9	X: 5)30 = 6	O: 12 ÷ 4 = 3

O: 28 ÷ 4 = 7	X: 5)30 = 6	O: 45 ÷ 5 = 9
X: 4)16 = 4	X: 32 ÷ 4 = 8	O: 5)15 = 3
O: 20 ÷ 4 = 5	X: 12 ÷ 3 = 4	X: 4)8 = 2

O: 5)25 = 5	X: 8 ÷ 4 = 2	X: 4)16 = 4
X: 32 ÷ 4 = 8	X: 5)20 = 4	O: 5)35 = 7
X: 5)40 = 8	O: 4)12 = 3	O: 15 ÷ 5 = 3

O: 36 ÷ 12 = 3	X: 9)18 = 2	X: 7)42 = 6
X: 2)12 = 6	O: 45 ÷ 9 = 5	X: 64 ÷ 8 = 8
O: 9)81 = 9	X: 24 ÷ 6 = 4	O: 7)49 = 7

Page 73

1. 63 ÷ 7 = 9; quotient = 9
2. 324 ÷ 2 = 162; divisor = 2
3. 49 ÷ 7 = 7; dividend = 49

Page 74

1. D
2. F
3. A
4. E
5. C
6. B